SONGS FOR ALL SORTS

compiled and edited by

Marion P. Prior

with illustrations by
Babs Sweet

1st Edition: 1990
2nd Edition: 1992
3rd Edition: 1994

Published by The Guide Association - Anglia Region
Ashley House, Old Station Road
Newmarket, CB8 8DT

ISBN. 0 9515862 0 3

Foreword

SONGS FOR ALL SORTS is the result of song gathering practised over a long period, waiting for the day I could put them together and publish them for the enjoyment of others.

I am very grateful to the many composers who gladly gave permission for their work to be published, and for the help and encouragement received from the Anglia Arts Team.

Mary Gentry and Janet Mackenzie were especially helpful, giving detailed study to the proofs and making most helpful suggestions about content and presentation. I'm grateful also to my colleague Paul Frecknall who designed the cover, to Babs Sweet who added her inimitable illustrations and to Carole Lindsay-Douglas who transformed aged, faded Bandas and manuscripts of the material into sparkling print with the aid of her clever computer, transforming a dream into reality.

Singers of many ages and abilities should find new material to suit them within these covers, and I hope Anglia (and others) will continue to make music in ALL SORTS of ways.

Marion P. Prior
Anglia Music Consultant

May 1990

Contents

Rainbows

Rainbow Guides Closing Song 3
Rainbow Guides Song 2

Brownies

Bim Bam Biri 6
Bless this house,
bless this food (Grace) 3
Scandinavian Prayer 4
That's the Brownie Way 5
Trulle and Trisse 6

Guides, Rangers and Young Leaders

Flicker 10
Have Fun! 12
Hey la-li-lo 11
Music Makers 7
Sing a Silly Song 9
Windmills 8
You Know We're All Feeling Happy 7

Rounds

Bellringer 14
Birthday Round 18
Come and Camp 18
Da-di-dah! 15
Feeling Free 19
In Athens 14
My Candle Burns 14
O Be Joyful 13
O Hark to the Lark 19
Round Without Words 19
Saamen Trekken 18
The Zoo 16

Part Songs

As We Trek Along 23
Look for the Beauty 30
Pilgrimage 20
Sing Round the Campfire 22
St Patrick's Breastplate 24
The River Runs High 28
Walking Song 26
Wind 21
Yulishka 29

Everyday is Thinking Day

Fiesta Song 32
He Puru Taitama 31
Japanese Drum Song 33
Lotus Flower 31
Pebbles 36
Sangam Festival Song 34
Song for Breaking the World Flag 38
Thinking Day '87 37
Think On 35

Dances and Singing Games

Ak Shav 40
Birthday Song 41
Estonian Arm Swinging 40
Hoida 39
Lapada 39
Marmee 42
Masilowe 42
Swedish Rhapsody 41
The Banks of the Hanky Panky 38

Two Descants

For the Beauty of the Earth 43
Thank-You 43

Christmas

Away in a Manger with obbligato 46
Away in a Manger for Bb instruments 47
Carillon - Round 44
Carol of the Field Mice 49
It's Christmas 48
Joseph and His Wife Mary 50
Mary's Lullaby 45
Prince of the Peasants - Round 44
Ting-a-ling-a-ling 50

Graces and Vespers

An Irish Blessing 53
An Old Sussex Grace 51
Cricket's Grace 51
God on High 52
Hautbois Vesper 54
Lord of the Night 54
Praise God for Sleep 53
The Friends Grace 52

RAINBOWS

Rainbow Guides Song

M.P.Prior

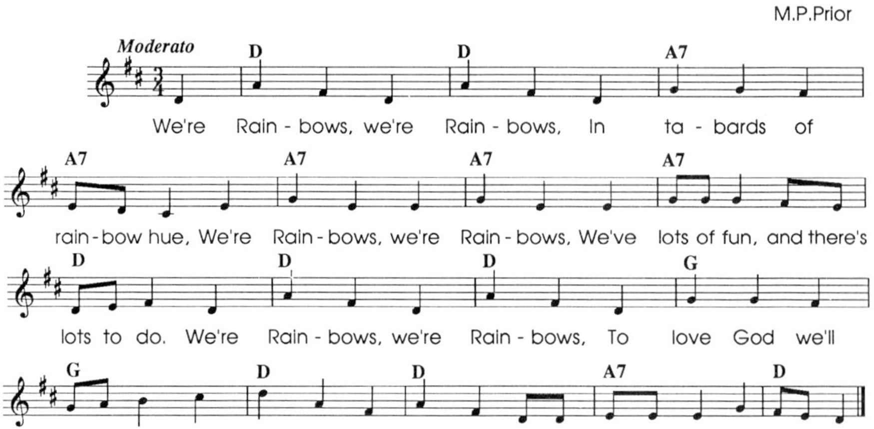

ACTIONS

We're Rainbows (twice)	Make rainbow shape in the air, once with each arm
In tabards.........	Show tabards by holding out in front
We're Rainbows (twice)	As first time
We've lots of fun	Clap rhythm of "lots of fun"
And there's lots to do	Stamp rhythm of "lots to do"
To love God................	Bring hands together as in prayer
Being kind and helpful	Join hands in a circle
till we rest	Head on hands together, as if asleep

Notes

1. Guitar or keyboard chords make an optional accompaniment.
2. The melody can be managed on a descant recorder to support the singing if required.
3. Repeated words such as "We're Rainbows" are a feature often found in songs for this age.
4. The words remind the children what being a Rainbow is about.
5. The word "hue" will probably need explanation, but is appropriate here, I feel.
6. The tune should not be hurried, as there are a lot of words to fit into some bars

   e.g. "lots of fun and there's | lots to do."

Rainbow Guides Closing Song

M.P.Prior

Notes
Three chime bars - middle C, D and E will make the simple accompaniment. Alternatively a child could use those notes on any pitched instrument, including piano or electronic keyboard.

BROWNIES

Bless this house, Bless this food

J. Richards

ACTIONS
1. Palms together, in prayer attitude
2. Hands raised, palm upwards, to side at shoulder height
3. As 1
4. Hands extended, palm downwards, over table
5. Left hand extended, palm up, towards neighbour
6. Right hand, palm down, placed into neighbour's hand
7. 8. All raise (now joined) hands in gesture of common worship.

Suitable for inter-racial or mixed religious groups as expressing gratitude to one God.

A grace written at Sangam, for Sangam.

Scandinavian Prayer

Tune from "Children's Songs of Iceland"
Translated by J. Froom

Part for Chime Bars - play in first four bars only (first and second times)

Note:
This tune is played on the Carillon at Pershore Abbey.
M.G.

From Music Workshop Book 2 arranged by K. Pont.
Reproduced by permission of Oxford University Press.

That's the Brownie Way

Isabel Brown

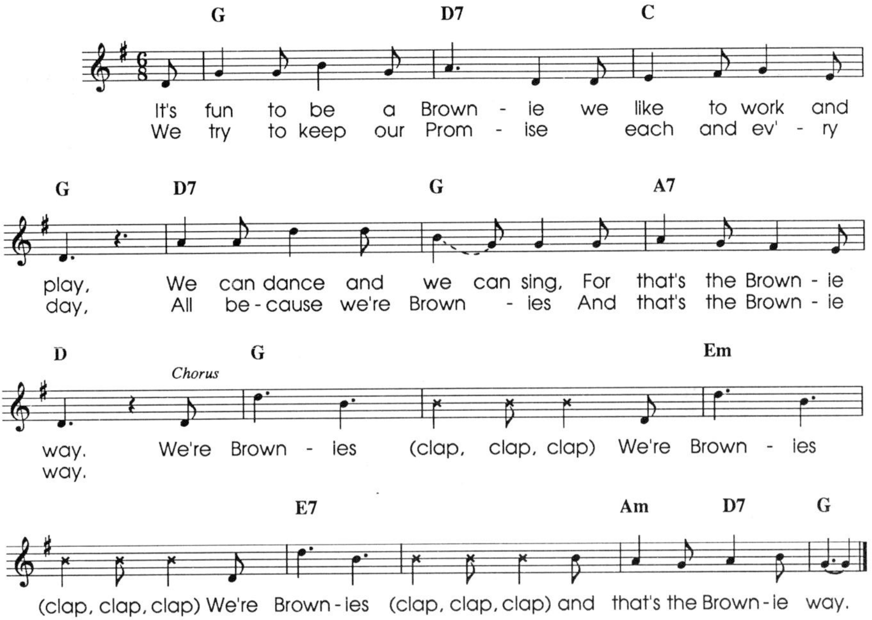

G D7 C

It's fun to be a Brown - ie we like to work and
We try to keep our Prom - ise each and ev' - ry

G D7 G A7

play, We can dance and we can sing, For that's the Brown - ie
day, All be - cause we're Brown - ies And that's the Brown - ie

D G Em

Chorus

way. We're Brown - ies (clap, clap, clap) We're Brown - ies
way.

E7 Am D7 G

(clap, clap, clap) We're Brown - ies (clap, clap, clap) and that's the Brown - ie way.

Used by permission

Trulle and Trisse

from Sweden

Notes
1. May be sung in 2 parts, 1st 4 bars against last 4 bars.
2, Alternative harmony for last 4 bars when singing in unison

G D^7 | D^7 G | Em Am | D^7 G ||

Bim Bam Biri

Yiddish

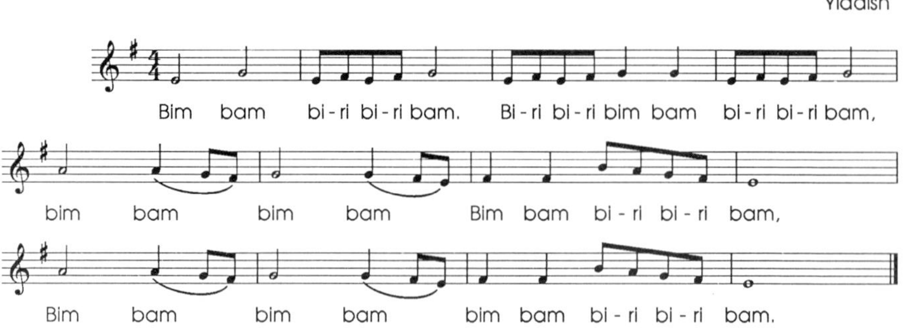

v.1. Bim - Slap own knees.
Bam - Slap neighbour's knees, each side.
Biri biri - Clap own hands twice.

v. 2. The same, but on Bam, clap hands with neighbours, R.H.up, L.H. down.

v. 3. The same, but on Bam, clap hands with neighbours, R.H. down, L.H. up.

GUIDES, RANGERS and YOUNG LEADERS

Music Makers

Words and Music by
A. and B. Buchanan and M.P. Prior

Used by permission. Written for Music Makers Camp 1966, Doe Lake, Canada.

You Know We're All Feeling Happy

Pat Durnall

2. You know we're all feeling happy when we click, etc.

3. You know we're all feeling happy when we sway, etc.

When the tune is well known, some singers may like to add their own harmony parts. M.P.

Used by permission

Windmills

Words and Music: Alan Bell

2
Through Flanders and Spain and the Lowlands of Holland,
Through the Kingdoms of England and Scotland and Wales,
Windmills grew up, all along the wild coast lines.
Ships of the land with their high canvas sails.
Chorus:

3
The Lancashire lads work hard with the good earth,
A-ploughing and sowing as the seasons declare,
Waiting to reap the rich golden harvest
While the miller, he idled his mill to repair.
Chorus:

4
Windmills so old, of wood blacked by weather,
Windmills of stone, glaring white in the sun,
Windmills like giants are ready for tilting,
Windmills that died in the gales and are gone.
Chorus:

Sing a Silly Song

Mary Gentry

D D A7 D
1.Sing a si - lly song, ________ Sing it right or sing it wrong.

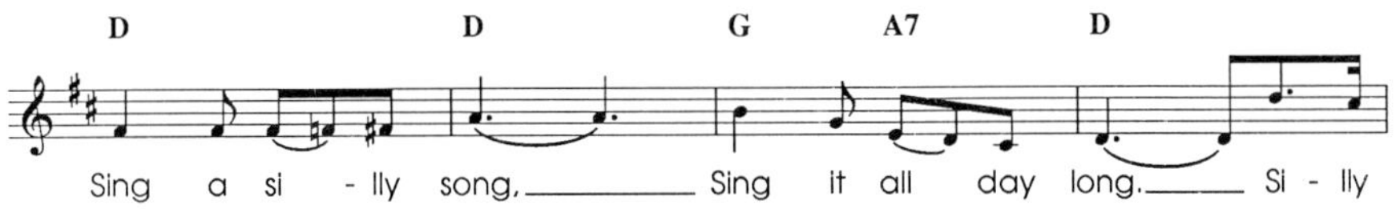

2. Sing an oom-pah-pah song, etc.

3. Sing a (make silly noise with fingers rubbing lips) song, etc.

Flicker

U.S.A.

This song has reached the U.K. orally without being committed to paper. This version was written down by Hettie Smith after some research in U.S.A. Various versions seem to harmonise with each other, and indeed this may be how differences have crept in. Let's not worry about them! M.P.

Hey la - li - lo

Source unknown

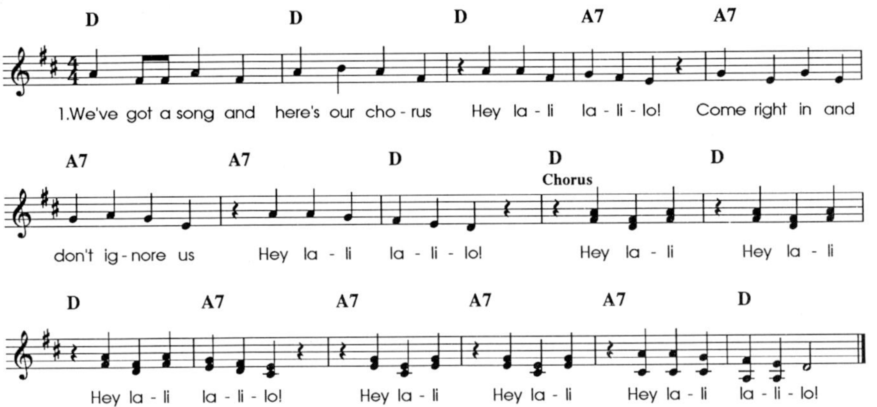

2
We've got a thought and here's our thesis:
Peace in the world or the world in pieces.
Chorus:

3
We've got a tale and here's our story
Hate brings death, but love brings glory.
Chorus:

4
We've got a dream and here's our dreaming
Trust in the world and no more scheming.
Chorus:

Have Fun!

U.S.A.: Source unknown

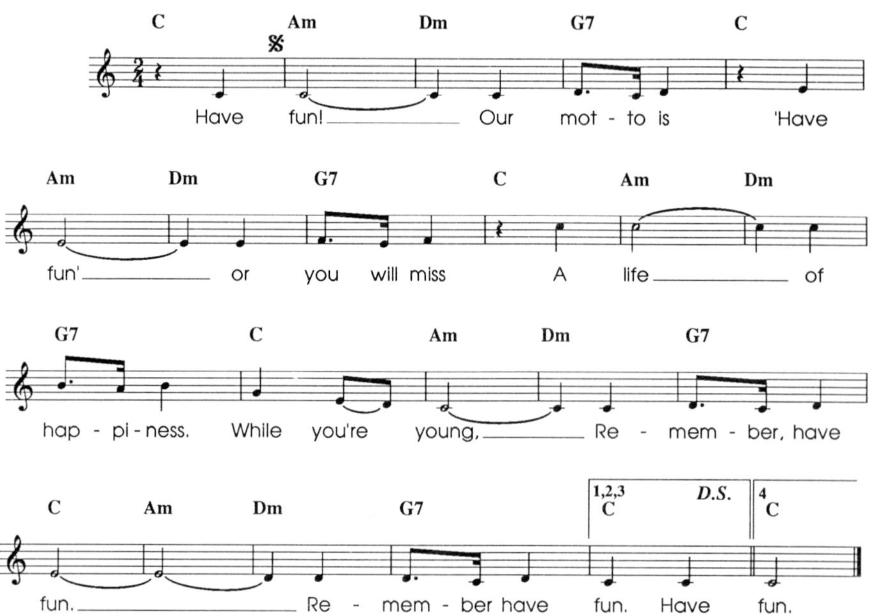

2
Have friends; believe in them,
Have friends; receive from them
A life of happiness. While you're young,
Remember, have fun. Remember, have fun.

3
Have faith in God above.
Have faith in His great love.
Have faith and happiness. While you're young,
Remember, have fun. Remember, have fun.

4
Have love; it's all that's good.
Have love; it's understood
You'll live the life you should. While you're young,
Remember, have fun. Remember, have fun.

ROUNDS

O Be Joyful

Three Part Round

U.S.A.: Source unknown

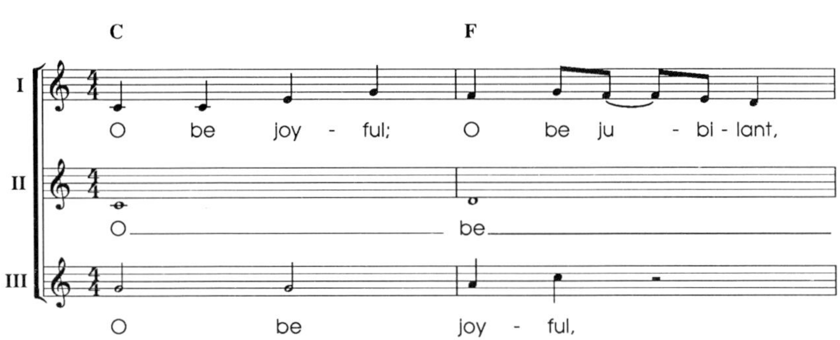

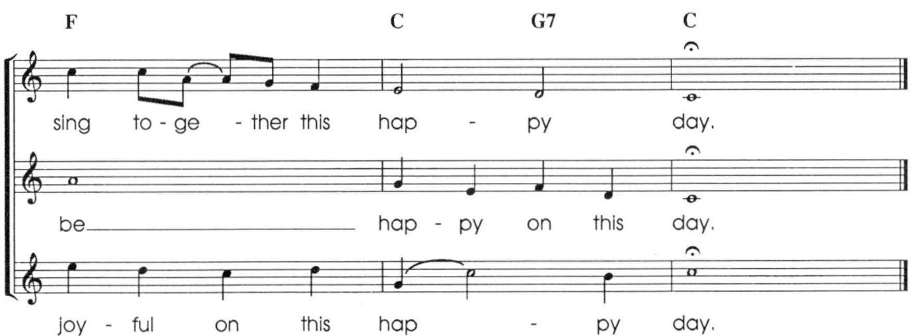

Bellringer

Words: Anon

Music: Traditional

My Candle Burns

Words: Edna St. Vincent Millay

Tune: Source unknown

In Athens

Pat Shaw

Note:
This round is not suitable for ending on a chord. Arrange for each part to sing through an agreed number of times. M.P.

Da - di - dah!

Words and Music: Sue Stevens

When both rounds are well known, The Zoo and Da-di-dah can be sung together.

Used by permission

The Zoo

Words and Music: Sue Stevens

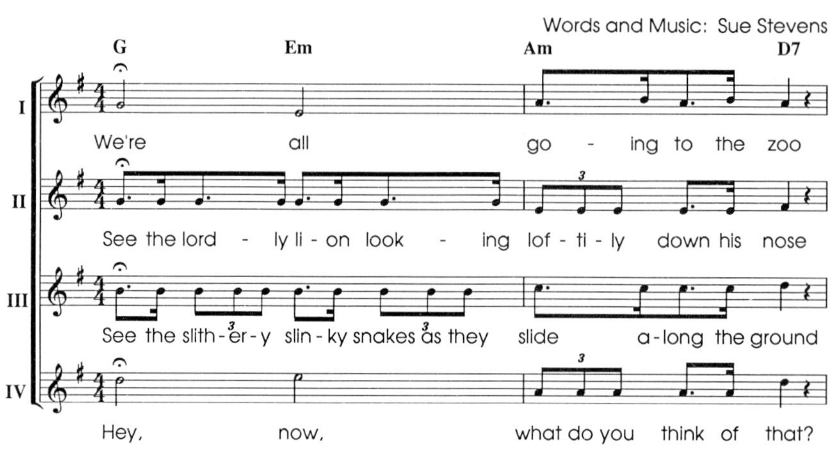

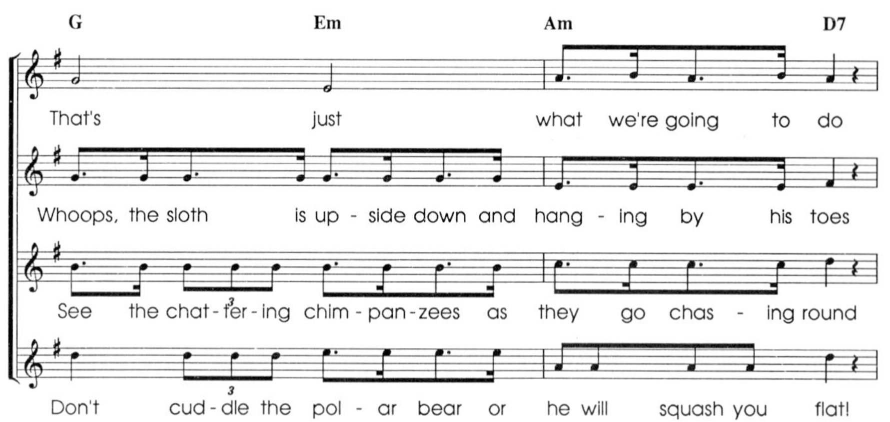

G Em Am D7

Catch the bus at half past two

Here's the craf - ty cro - co - dile, he's hav - ing a lit - tle doze

Hear the cack - l - ing cock - a - too, Oh what an aw - ful sound.

This friend - ly tig - er's not a pus - sy cat!

D7 D7

We're all go - ing to the zoo.

There are lots of an - i - mals at the zoo.

It's all hap - pen - ing at the zoo.

You can get eat - en at the zoo.

Used by permission.

Saamen Trekken

Afrikaans

Birthday Round

M. Hauptmann

It would be best to let each part sing to the end. Stopping on a chord would be hazardous! M.P.

Come and Camp

Alternative words: M. Prior and M. Gentry

Melody: Pat Shaw

Originally this tune was sung to 'lah'. Some words have been suggested. Can you invent any for yourselves?

Feeling Free

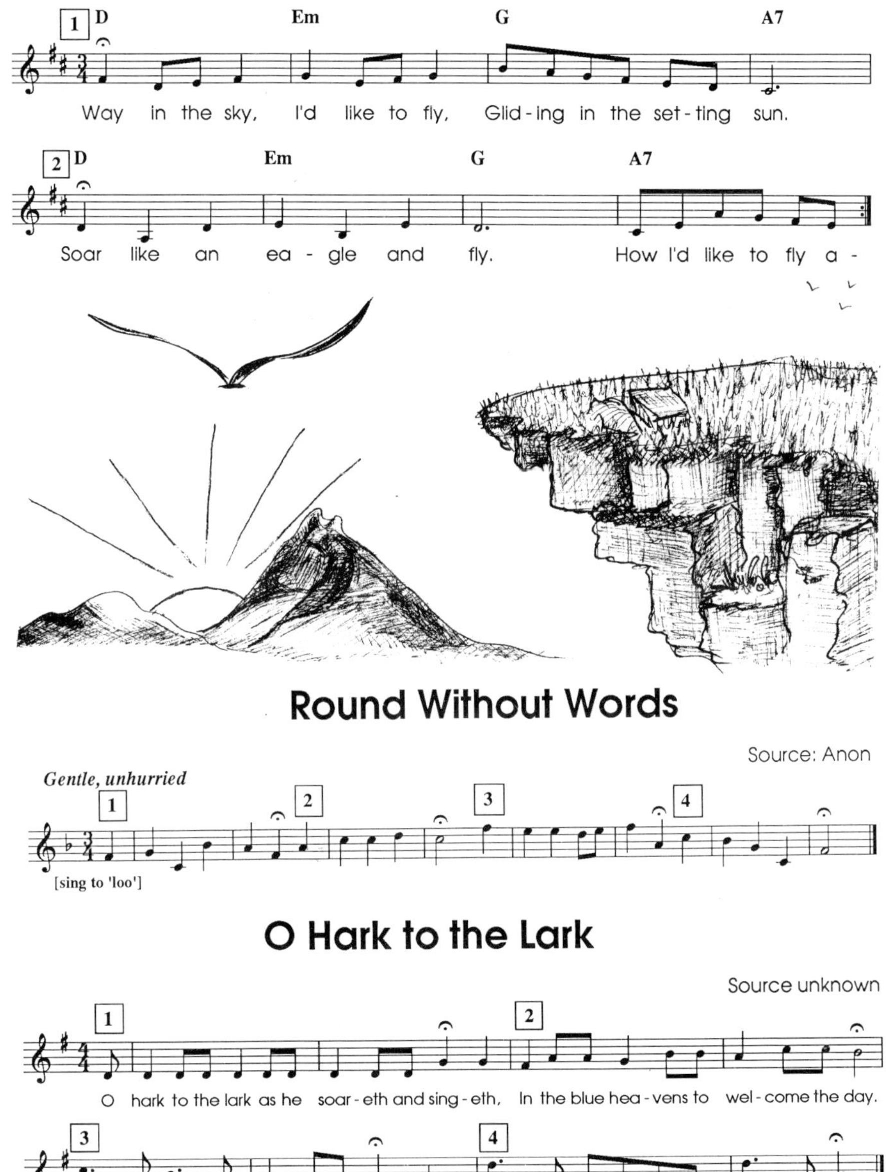

Words: Lloyd Poole and friends

Music: Lloyd Poole (Victoria, Aust.)

1 D Em G A7

Way in the sky, I'd like to fly, Glid - ing in the set - ting sun.

2 D Em G A7

Soar like an ea - gle and fly. How I'd like to fly a -

Round Without Words

Source: Anon

Gentle, unhurried

1 2 3 4

[sing to 'loo']

O Hark to the Lark

Source unknown

1 2

O hark to the lark as he soar - eth and sing - eth, In the blue hea - vens to wel - come the day.

3 4

Joy - ful - ly, re - veil - le he fling - eth, Sweet his car - ol - ing and clear his lay.

PART SONGS

Pilgrimage

M.P.Prior © 1984

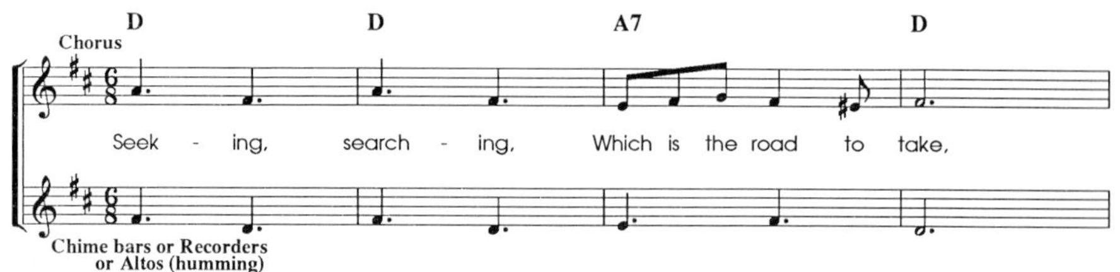

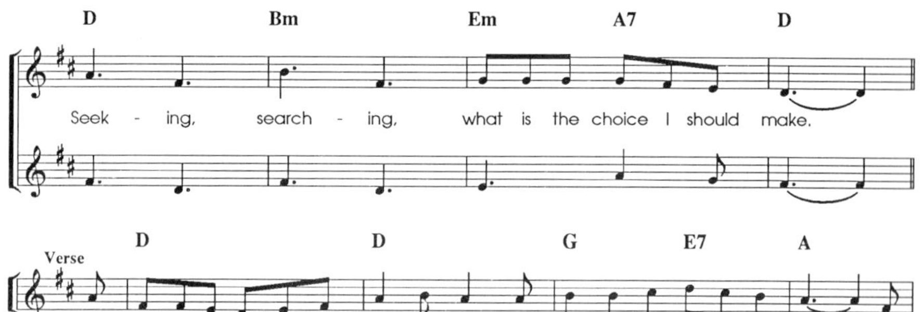

2
To help on our journey we've friends you know,
Who travel the road as well,
And leaders and teachers who show us how
We have the wrong to quell.

3
It's Gods highway we travel along,
His Word will be our guide,
Our footsteps He knows and joy He bestows
As we travel with Him to bide.

Wind

Words for verse 1: John Galsworthy

Music: Marie Gaudette
Arranged by Christine Trevor

Used by permission from Marie Gaudette's Songs.

Extra verses written by Di Stagg at the launch of "Songs for All Sorts" 12th May, 1990.

Sing Round the Campfire

Words and Music: Daphne Bird

G G
With a swing

La la la la la la la etc.

2
Sing round the campfire; trees overhead
Arching above us, with boughs outspread;
Guides the world over, with hearts that are gay
Sing round their campfire, at the end of the day.

3
Sing round the campfire; now flames burn low,
Sing our last song, ere to rest we go;
This we are certain, all through the night
God will keep us, till morning light.

As We Trek Along

Arranged by Christine Trevor

Used by permission - The Girl Guides Association (U.K.)

St. Patrick's Breastplate

Music: Mary Chater

Used by permission.

Walking Song

Words and Music: W. H. Neidlinger

Formerly published in Kent County Song Book

The River Runs High

Boardman and Landis

Published by Holt, Rinehart & Winston Inc. Used by permission.

Yulishka

Czech folk tune
Words and arrangement
by R. Sabor

1.Yul-ish-ka un-der the li-lac tree Oh Fa-ria, fa -ri - a, Yul-ish-ka where my

heart must be, Oh Fa - ria, fa -ri - a, Don't cast down your eyes so bright,

Come and dance with me to-night, Fa-ri-a, Fa-ri-a, Fa-ri-a, Fa-ri-a, Fa - ri - a.

2
Gypsy maidens are proud and free
Oh Faria, faria,
Leave me under the lilac tree
Oh Faria, faria,
Tell me laddie, tell me true
Wherefore should I dance with you?
Faria, Faria, Faria, Faria,
Faria.

3
Moth and glow worm wing the air
Oh Faria, faria,
Star swept wind caress your hair
Oh Faria, faria,
Hear the music from my guitar,
Clash your cymbals Yulishka.
Faria, Faria, Faria, Faria,
Faria.

Look for the Beauty

Words and Melody : Anne Mcgregor
Arrangement : Heather J. Reed 1985

2
Look for the music in sounds that you hear;
Bird song at morning, the stream rippling clear,
Laughter of children, the hum of the bee;
Look for it, seek, you will find it.

3
Look for the wonder of things great and small;
Love of our Father, who cares for us all,
Pattern of seasons, the joy of new birth,
Look for it, seek, you will find it.

Used by permission

"EVERY DAY IS THINKING DAY"

Lotus Flower

Buddhist Prayer Wheel Song

Traditional

Buddhist Prayer Wheel: ACTIONS

1st time go round with hand to show wheel movement.

2nd time slowly open and close hands to represent the opening and closing of the beautiful lotus flower.

He Puru Taitama

Maori (New Zealand)

In Maori, vowels are pronounced "a" as in rather, "e" as in pleasure, "i" as in teem, "o" as or, "u" as in tube while consonants are pronounced as in English . Note that each syllable ends in a vowel. The alphabet only has a, e, h, i, k, m, n, o, p, r, t, u, and w. The "f" sound is given by wh. The true spelling, and the meaning of the words has only recently been discovered through the research of Hettie Smith, and her contact with a New Zealand trainer. They mean: "What a fine bull you are, a mighty fine bull, a rushing bull! What a bull you are.

Here is another example of a song travelling in the oral tradition, and, like Chinese whispers, changing on the way. I learned this as a Guide, but my research for the first edition bore no fruit, since I was asking the wrong questions.

MPP June 1994

Fiesta Song

Mexican

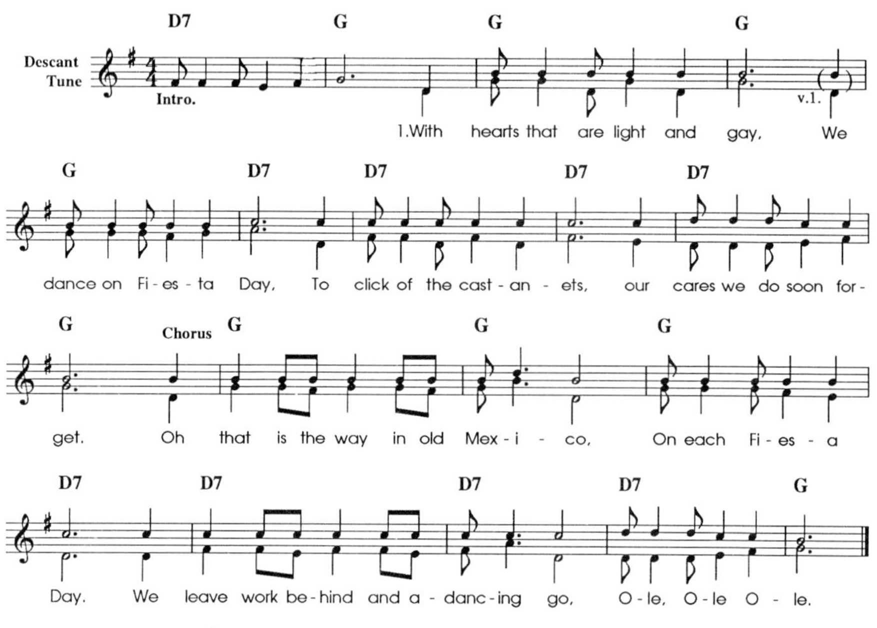

2
Oh how the guitars do play, on our Fiesta Day,
To jingle of tambourine, we dance on the village green.
Chorus:

Adapted from a Mexican Dance - La Raspa

Japanese Drum Song

Traditional Japanese

O Ki Na Ta - i - ko Don Don Ti Sa Na Ta - i - ko Ton Ton Ton

O Ki Na Ta - i - ko Ti Sa Na Ta - i - ko Don Don Ton Ton Ton.

O Ki Na = Big
Ti Sa Na = Little
Taiko = Drum

Notes
Try also:
O Ki Na enu = Big dog
O Ki Na tori = Big bird
O Ki Na nayko = Big cat
and make appropriate noises for the animals instead of the drum sounds.

Sangam Festival Song

© Sue Wingfield

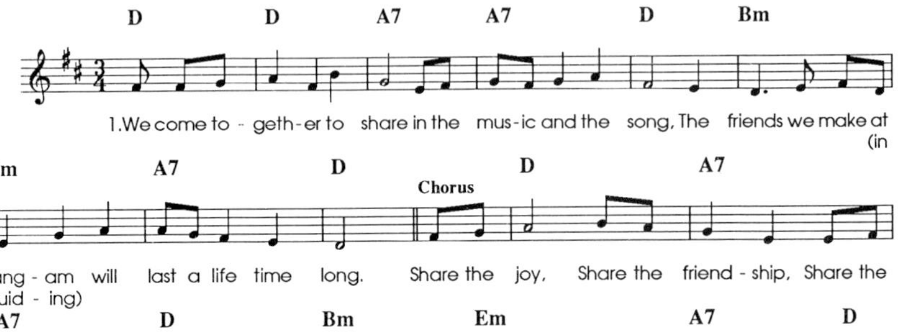

2
We share the laughter and joy,
All our cares and sorrows gone.
United in our music,
At Sangam (in Guiding) we are one.
Chorus:

Used by permission

Think On

Rita and Sally Sandifer © 1978

Used by permission

Pebbles

U.S.A. : Source unknown

G C D7
1.One lit - tle peb - ble and the cir - cles be - gin, a cir - cle in a cir - cle, they go

G G C D7
on with - out end. Rip - ples on the wa - ter move a - cross the pond, The peb - ble dis - ap - pears but the

D7 G G Am
Chorus
cir - cles move a - long. Cir - cles on wa - ter from one lit - tle stone, The

D G G Am
wa - ter is smooth if you leave it a - lone, Each peb - ble you toss makes a diff' - rence you see, The

D7 1 D7 G D.S. 2 D7 G
rip - ples of cir - cles can touch both you and me. Touch both you and me.

2
Pebbles of good and pebbles of bad,
Circles of happiness and circles of sad,
No way to stop them once they begin,
So stop and think a minute,
Then toss your pebble in.
Chorus:

Thinking Day '87

by Maureen E. Channon

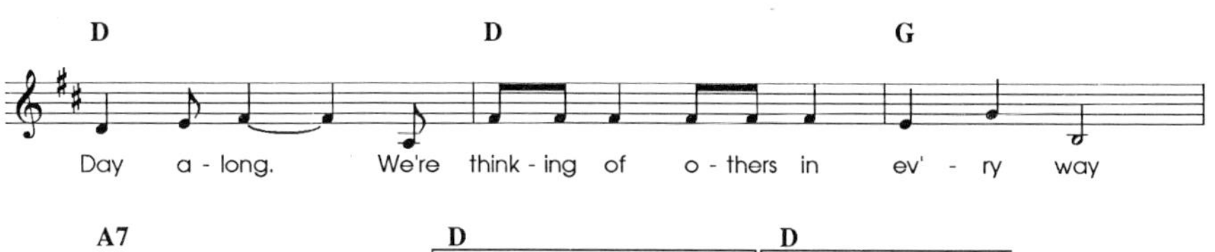

2
Let's join together in this simple song
Its Tra la la la la helps Thinking Day along
Today round the world we will tour
To India, Canada and Singapore.

3
Let's join together in this simple song
Its Tra la la la la helps Thinking Day along
We've tried to yodel like a well tuned band
But we'll leave it to our sisters in Switzerland.

4
Let's join together in this simple song
Its Tra la la la la helps Thinking Day along
We dream by the campfire wishing we could go
And visit Our Cabana in Mexico.

5
Let's join together in this simple song
It's Tra la la la la helps Thinking Day along
In Kenya our animals are well preserved
On land which for them is specially reserved.

6
Let's join together in this simple song
Its Tra la la la la helps Thinking Day along
We are like the links in a very strong chain
And join with our sisters in sunny Spain.

7
Let's join together in this simple song
Its Tra la la la la helps Thinking Day along
Windmills in Holland turn around in the breeze
Showing friendship to others comes with great ease.

8
Let's join together in this simple song
Its Tra la la la la helps Thinking Day along
To keep our promise we are glad
And salute with fellow Guides in Trinidad

Used by permission.

Song for Breaking the World Flag

Jane Robinson

Used by permission

DANCES AND SINGING GAMES

The Banks of the Hanky Panky

From the U.S.A.

Formation: STAND IN A CIRCLE

1. Right foot out to right and back (4 times).
2. Feet together, jump left, back, right and forward.
3. a) hands up in front, palms forward, as knees bend.
   b) hands down (knees bent, palms in) straighten up.
4. Hands up (shoulder height), fingers up, and shake, while turning once on spot.
5. Slap knees.
6. Clap hands.

Hoida

Finnish Washerwomen's Dance

DANCE

Stand in a close circle. Join hands thus:-
Extend right hand and put in front of right hand neighbour. Extend left hand over arm in front of you and join up with right hand of next door but one person on the left.

1. Stand on left leg and point right foot in front.
2. Stand on left leg and point right foot to right side.
3. Stand on left leg and point right foot to back.
4. Bring right foot next to left and stamp. Repeat 1 to 4.
5. Stamp right foot.
6. Stamp left foot.
7. Cross right foot in front of left and kick left up behind, leaning forward and putting weight on right.
8. Tip back on to the left foot.

Repeat 7 and 8 to end of tune.
When all are "in step" whole circle moves to the left whilst keeping 7 and 8 going.

Notes:
a) Should look like a wash dolly in the tub!
b) Three times through is usually enough to bring on exhaustion, or to warm parts that heating cannot reach!

M.P.

Lapada

Singing Game

Danish

DANCE

Circle formation - hold hands 1st time -
take 4 side-together steps to the left, then 4 to the right.
Repeat for each verse with hands on the appropriate place on your neighbours' bodies, according to the question and answer with the Leader.
Leader: "Have you danced with your hands on your heads"?
(shoulders/waists/knees/ankles)

Group: "No" (or "Yes" as appropriate).
Leader: "Then let's!"
Put hands on neighbours heads etc., and repeat the dance.
The Leader asks the questions, starting with the head each time and working through the list until she receives the answer "No".

Estonian Arm Swinging

Traditional

Formation:
Longways set, couples holding hands across set.

A

Swing arms side to side. Do this between each verse.

B

Verses - sing as many times as necessary.
1st verse: Hold inner hands; top couple face rest of set, who make arches. Top couple go down set under arches, as arches move towards top of set. At bottom of set, they turn and make an arch and walk back to place.
i.e. If moving down set, go under arches. If moving up set, make arches.
All couples do same.

2nd verse: As for 1st verse, but couples alternately go under an arch, then make an arch for next couple. "Dip and Dive" down and up set till all get back to places.

3rd verse: Hold both hands across, facing inwards. First couple move out to side of set and in again, with shunting movement, passing a couple on the way who are shunting in the opposite direction. Shunt to other side to pass next couple. Couples join in as 1st couple reaches them. At ends of set wait for one shunt, then join in as appropriate to the approaching couple. Keep going until all are back to original places.

Ak Shav

(Welcome to Israel)

Traditional

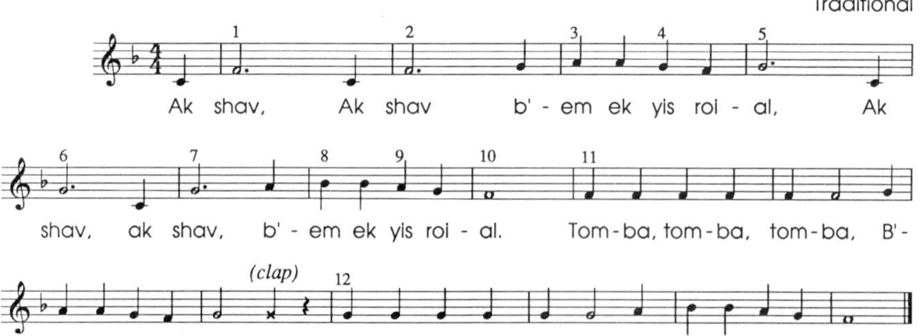

Formation
A circle, with partners side by side.

1. Point right heel into circle. Spring and change to 2.
2. Point left heel into circle.
3. to 10. Continue alternating between right and left heel.
11. Link right arms with partner and swing, stepping in time with the singing and clap hands on "Hey!" Change arms just before,
12. Link left arms and swing together the other way.

Return to circle formation for further "verses" until breath runs out!

Swedish Rhapsody

Action Song

ACTIONS
1. Tap knees twice.
2. Clap hands twice.
3. L.H. points R. twice.
4. R.H. points L. twice.
5. Touch R. elbow twice.
6. Touch L. elbow twice.
7. Wave L. hand.
8. Wave R. hand.

Repeat above four times.
Increase speed as you sing through again.

Three times is usually enough for all to "catch on".

M.P.

Birthday Song

Afrikaans

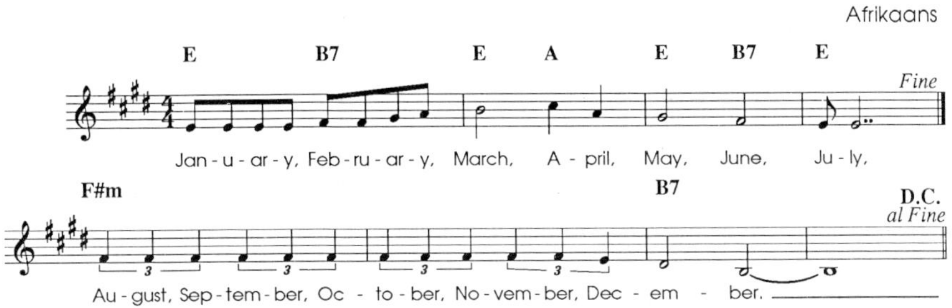

Make a game of this by asking singers to stand up when it is their birthday month, as you sing it through the first time. Sit at the same month as it is sung for the second time. You'll have to sing January to July a third time to finish off the tune - see who can remember not to stand up again!
This is fun for all ages, and works well on big occasions.

M. P.

Masilowe

Lesotho

FORMATION
Circle of partners, one with back to centre, the other facing the centre.
ACTION
1. Clap own knees
2. Clap own hands
3. Clap R.H. with partner's R.H.
4. Clap L.H. with partner's L.H.

Repeat to end. After each time through, outside circle progresses one place to right, inner circle stays still. If you have time, continue until you have clapped with everyone in the outer circle.
PRONUNCIATION
Mar - see - low - ay, hay la mar see-low etc.

Marmee

a clapping game

African

Formation

Players should stand in a circle, R.H. facing down, L.H. facing up, resting (RH) supporting (LH) neighbours' hands, forming a continuous circle of touching hands.

1. Tap on neighbours' hands.
2. Clap own hands together, keeping R.H. palm down, L.H. palm up. Repeat for four bars. (Say "out, in out, in" to help learning).
3. Tap on neighbours' hands.
4. Clap own hands together as before.
5. and 6. Repeat 3. and 4.
7. Reverse own hands and tap neighbours' hands and immediately turn back again to starting position. You should end with your own hands together!

Notes
This was taught to an English trainer by Mrs. Ampopho who was attending a training in the U.K.

TWO HYMN DESCANTS

Descant - For the Beauty of the Earth

[England's Lane]

M.P. Prior 1984

Descant - Thank-you

M.P. Prior

Ah Ah etc.

Written for Thinking Day service in Westminster Abbey, 1980

Original melody by Martin G. Schneider may be found in Faith Folk and Clarity p.3, or Youth Praise I no.13.

CHRISTMAS

Prince of the Peasants

by Siân Howell-Pryce

This round would probably be best sung through an agreed number of times for each part. As each finishes, continue repeating part 4 until all are singing the final 'Hallelujah'.
Used by permission

Carillon

M. Chater

Used by permission

Mary's Lullaby

Polish Carol arranged by
J.A.Ireland © 1982

Used by permission.

Note: Guitar chords and piano harmonies are non-compatible.
Use only one at a time! M.P.

Away in a Manger

Words: Anon

Melody: W.J. Kirkpatrick
Arranged by Marion P. Prior

Obbligato for Flute or Descant Recorder

G D7 G G E7 Am

1.A - way in a man - ger, no crib for a bed, The

D7 G A7 D D7

lit - tle Lord Je - sus laid down his sweet head. The

G D7 G G E7 Am

stars in the bright sky looked down where he lay, The

D G C Am D7 G

lit - tle Lord Je - sus a - sleep on the hay.

2
The cattle are lowing, the baby awakes,
But little Lord Jesus no crying he makes.
I love thee, Lord Jesus! Look down from the sky,
And stay by my side until morning is nigh.

3
Be near me Lord Jesus; I ask thee to stay
Close by me for ever, and love me, I pray.
Bless all the dear children in thy tender care,
And fit us for heaven, to live with thee there.

Away in a Manger

(for Bb Instruments e.g. clarinet/cornet/trumpet)

It's Christmas

Maureen Channon

Used by permission.

Carol of the Field Mice

Words from "Wind in the Willows"
by Kenneth Grahame

Music: Linda Hewitt

Used by permission.

Ting-a-Ling-a-Ling

by Maureen Channon

2
Ting-a-ling-a-ling say the Christmas bells,
From ev'ry church tower their music swells,
Peace and joy throughout the land
Joining us together in this happy band.

3
Ting-a-ling-a-ling say the Christmas bells,
From ev'ry church tower their music swells,
Good will to everyone assembled here
Happy Christmas and a good New Year.

Used by permission.

Joseph and His Wife Mary

by Maureen Channon

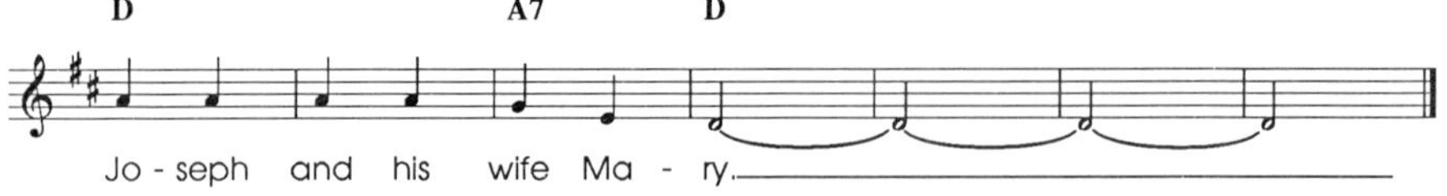

2
Three, four, five, six,
Who is it that's in a fix
Joseph and his wife Mary.

3
Five, six, seven, eight
What is there to celebrate
With Joseph and his wife Mary.

4
Seven, eight, nine, ten,
Here come the three wise men
Seeking Joseph and his wife Mary.

5
Joseph and Mary are full of joy
Jesus Christ
Is their baby boy.

Used by permission

GRACES AND VESPERS

An Old Sussex Grace

Words: Traditional

Music: Sue Stevens

The Old Sussex Grace "Bees of Paradise" has been enjoyed by many since it was first published, but the meaning of the words has always needed a bit of explaining. The following extract, sent to Hettie Smith by Janet Wood (nee Cozens), throws a whole new light on the probable source of the words.

M.P.

Extract from "Early to Rise" by Bob Cooper, about his early life in Rottingdean, Sussex.

Through the polished panes of narrow casements wrapped with white lace curtains, cats could be seen curled up asleep beside the potted cyclamen or geranium which, in many cases, shared the window-sill with jam-jars full of pale, yellowish liquid in which small blobs of yeast culture surfaced and sank with monotonous regularity like restless balls of cotton wool. This was 'bee-wine' in the making and so called because the fluffy pieces of yeast were known as 'Jerusalem bees'. They were 'fed' on sugar and after a week or two in a warm window, the water, with which the process had been started, was miraculously turned into wine, and all for the price of a few spoonfuls of sugar. It was a craze that swept the southern counties in the twenties and, in fact, 'bee-wine', I think, was known throughout the country".

Cricket's Grace

Lura Collier, Texas

May also be used at Colours, or a Flag Ceremony.

God on High

R. Sandifer

Used by permission.

The Friend's Grace

Marion P. Prior

Written for the first Friends of Hautbois weekend, October 1988.

An Irish Blessing

Words: Gaelic

arr. Foxlease Singing Circle
Tune from U.S.A.

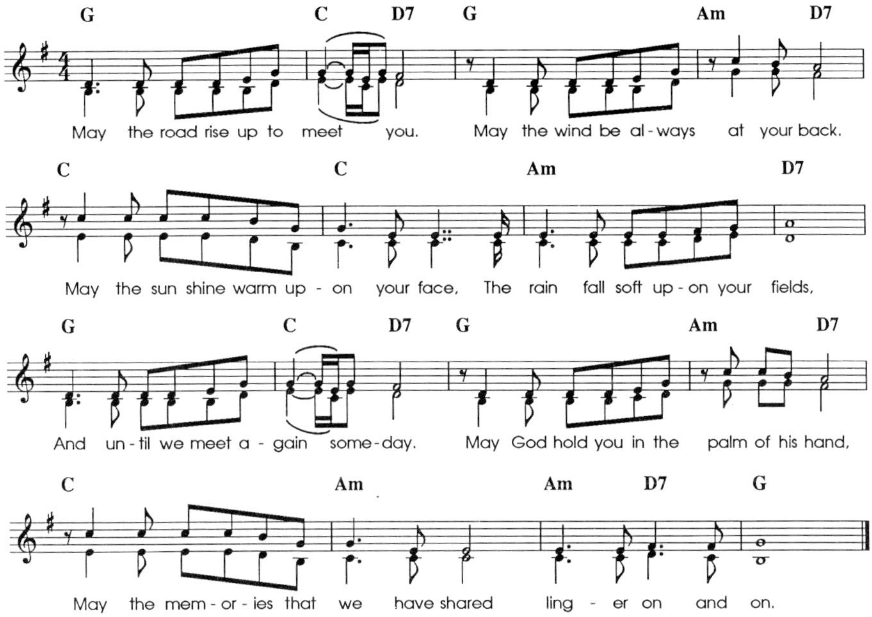
G C D7 G Am D7
May the road rise up to meet you. May the wind be al-ways at your back.
C C Am D7
May the sun shine warm up - on your face, The rain fall soft up - on your fields,
G C D7 G Am D7
And un-til we meet a - gain some-day. May God hold you in the palm of his hand,
C Am Am D7 G
May the mem-or-ies that we have shared ling - er on and on.

Praise God for Sleep

Source unknown

Praise God for sleep in the cool qui - et night, Praise God for the
sun's re - turn - ing light; For health and food and
strength to run in the wind and the wea-ther and the morn - ing sun.

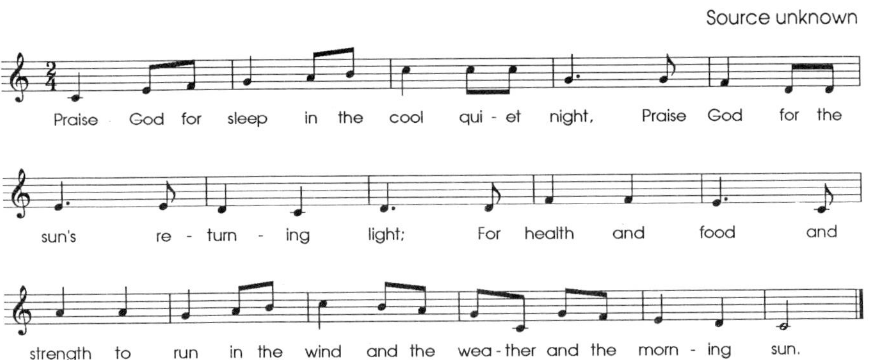

Hautbois Vesper

Words and music: M.P.Prior © 1988

Written for the Opening of Hautbois House, May 1988.

Note:
Guitar chords are provided only for use when the Vesper is being sung in Unison. M.P.

Lord of the Night

Di Stagg

Each part enters at 2 bar intervals, and continues singing until fourth part has been sung twice. Then sing Coda.

M.P.

Written during an Anglia Craft Weekend at Wantage, June 1989. Used by permission

GUITAR CHORDS

used to accompany songs in this book

Major Chords | **Minor Chords** | **7th Chords**

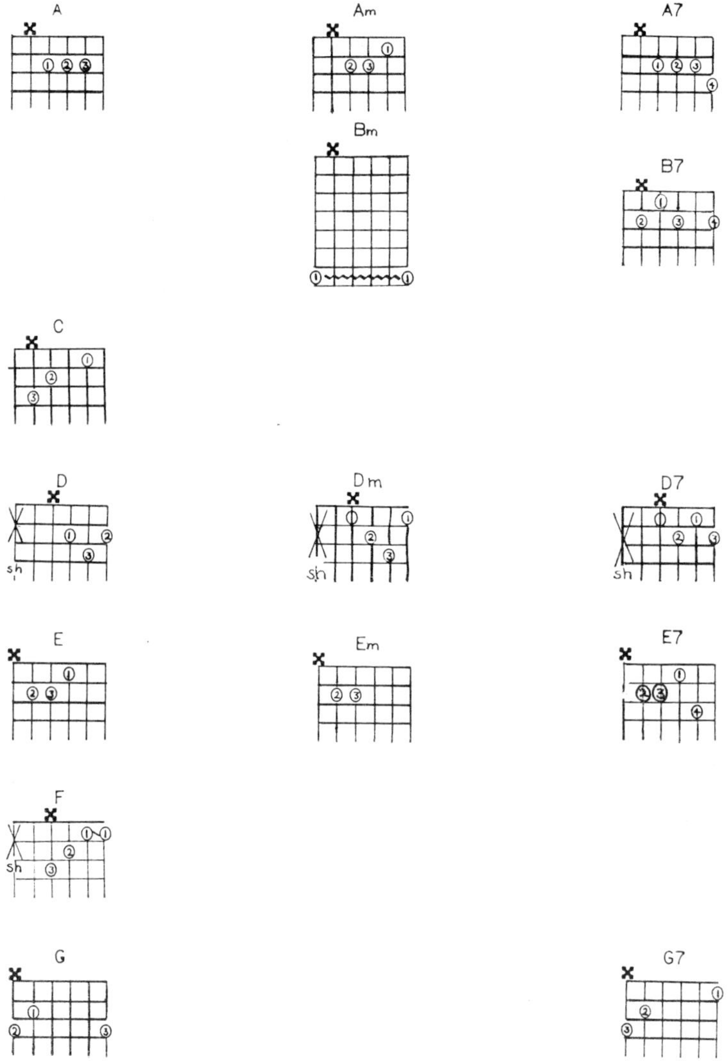

A

Am

A7

Bm

B7

C

D

Dm

D7

sh

E

Em

E7

F

sh

G

G7

Guitarists may wish to add their own chord fingertips for other songs within the spaces left above. String marked X should be the lowest note played.